Opportunities Matter

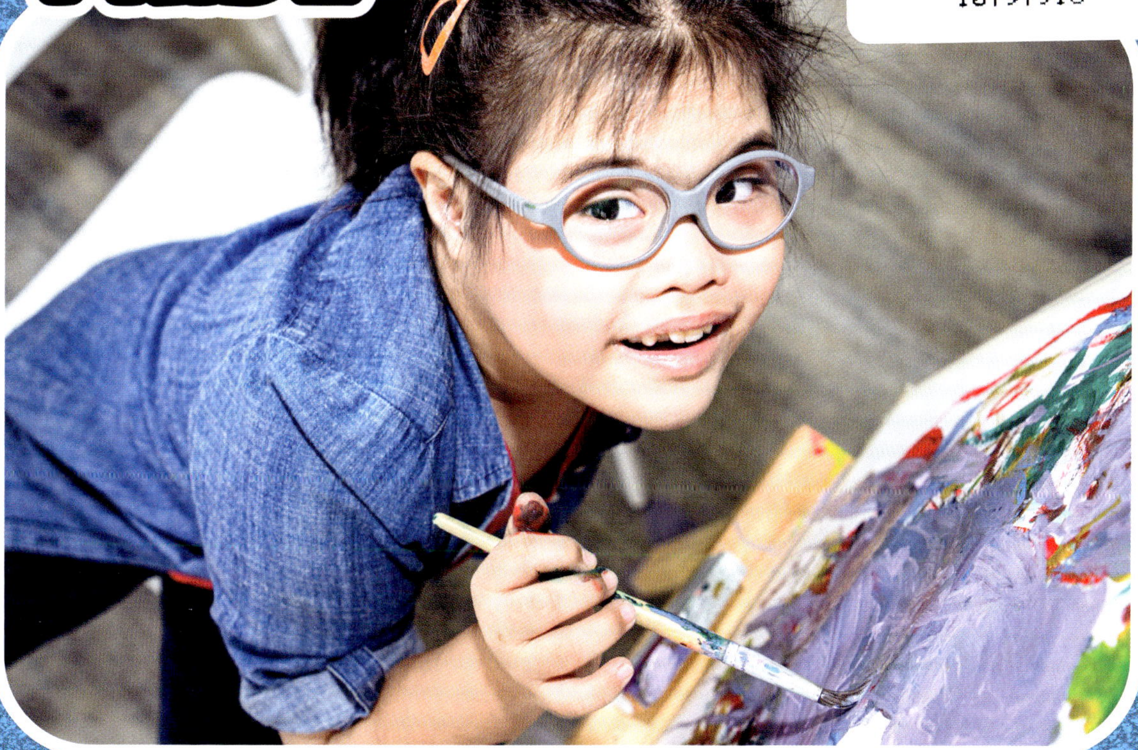

Jeni Vasquez

PowerKiDS press

Published in 2026 by The Rosen Publishing Group, Inc.
2544 Clinton Street, Buffalo, NY 14224

First Edition

Editor: Danielle Haynes
Book Design: Leslie Taylor

Photo Credits: Cover Manop Boonpeng/Shutterstock.com; (series background) P.siripak/Shutterstock.com; (series disability pride colors) rudall30/Shutterstock.com; p. 5 AnnGaysorn/Shutterstock.com; p. 5 (flag sidebar) Maxim Studio/Shutterstock.com; p. 7 Harbucks/Shutterstock.com; p. 9 Hryshchyshen Serhii/Shutterstock.com; p. 11 BAZA Production/Shutterstock.com; p. 12 Reshetnikov_art/Shutterstock.com; p. 13 VectorMine/Shutterstock.com; p. 15 U.S. Department of State/Flickr.com; p. 17 Juice Verve/Shutterstock.com; p. 19 Dikushin Dmitry/Shutterstock.com; p. 21 Viktor Lom/iStockphoto.com.

Cataloging-in-Publication Data

Names: Vasquez, Jeni.
Title: Opportunities matters / Jeni Vasquez.
Description: Buffalo, New York : PowerKids Press, 2026. | Series: Disability pride | Includes glossary and index.
Identifiers: ISBN 9781499457063 (pbk.) | ISBN 9781499457070 (library bound) | ISBN 9781499457087 (ebook)
Subjects: LCSH: People with disabilities–Civil rights–United States–Juvenile literature. | People with disabilities–Legal status, laws, etc.–United States–Juvenile literature. | Discrimination against people with disabilities–United States–Juvenile literature. | People with disabilities–Juvenile literature.
Classification: LCC HV1553.V38 2026 | DDC 362.40973-dc23

Manufactured in the United States of America

Some of the images in this book illustrate individuals who are models. The depictions do not imply actual situations or events.

CPSIA Compliance Information: Batch #CWPK26. For Further Information contact Rosen Publishing at 1-800-237-9932.

Contents

A Chance to Shine

An opportunity is a good chance to do something, but often, it's not as simple as it sounds! Say you have an opportunity to take a class on a subject you love. But what if you use a wheelchair, and the class is in a building without **access** for it? What if you have a learning difference, but there are no **accommodations** in place to help you in this class? Is this an opportunity at all in these cases?

Sometimes, things need to be a little different to give everyone the opportunities they need to learn, live, work, and play. All kinds of people deserve the chance to shine!

The disability pride flag was created to show acceptance and respect for people who have disabilities. Each color is for a different type of disability.

- The gray background is in honor of those who've died.
- Green is for disabilities that have to do with the senses.
- Blue is for those that have to with the mind and emotions.
- White stands for unseen disabilities, as well as those that haven't been diagnosed, or found out.
- Gold is for **neurodiversity**.
- Red is for other disabilities of the body.

A wheelchair can mean freedom to someone with mobility, or movement, issues.

Fighting for Rights

People with disabilities and their **allies** have worked for their rights for a long time. In the past, many people didn't think that those with disabilities had the same right to things other people had, such as access to jobs, housing, and other basic human rights and opportunities.

There are now laws in the United States that protect some rights of people with disabilities. But there are still many issues, and many people worry that laws could change again. Standing up for your rights and those of others is very important. The most important U.S. law affecting those with disabilities is the Americans with Disabilities Act (ADA).

What if this was the only way to get into your school, but you or a friend used a wheelchair? Even a few steps can be an issue!

Learn More

The ADA became law in the United States on July 26, 1990. It was amended, or changed, in 2008.

The ADA

The ADA is very important when it comes to opportunities for those with disabilities. These opportunities including jobs, **transportation**, and many government services. Some notable parts of the act say that businesses or other **employers** can't refuse to hire someone for a job just because they have a disability. They must provide them what they need to do that job.

The ADA also says that public buildings and places must also be accessible to people with disabilities. They must be able to get inside and use any services there. This can mean things such as ramps, or slopes, for wheelchairs. But it means more than that too!

Ramps aren't the only thing that needs to be considered for wheelchair users. Doorways need to be wide enough for a chair to pass. It doesn't help to get into a building if you can't get into any rooms!

Learn More

According to the ADA, wheelchair ramps must have a slope of no more than 1:12, which is 1 inch (2.5 cm) of rise for each 12 inches (30.5 cm) of ramp length. For steeper slopes, a building or area might need an elevator.

Equality, Equity

It's easy to think that the goal for everyone, including the many people with different disabilities, is equality. However, equity is a better target. With equality, everyone is treated exactly the same. But this doesn't always work when people need different things.

Imagine three people trying to pick some fruit from a tall tree. One is tall enough to reach it on their own. The second is a bit too short. They could use a boost, or lift, to reach the fruit. The third is much shorter and would need a bigger boost to reach anything at all. Only one person has the opportunity to pick the fruit.

It's important to remember that many disabilities are invisible. You can't see them. This could be true of anyone around you, including your friends and classmates.

Learn More

Braille is a writing system used by people who are blind. There are Braille displays and keyboards that can be connected to computers.

You could say that with equality, these three people are each given a box of an equal height to stand on. But the tall person doesn't need the box. The middle person now can reach, but the shortest person still can't.

With equity, every person gets a box that meets their needs. The tall person doesn't get one. The middle person gets a box that lifts them the right amount, and so does the shortest person. Like this, every person with a disability needs the boost that's right for them. That might be a wheelchair ramp. It could also be a Braille keyboard (pictured below) or many other things!

Think of the tree's fruit as opportunities of all kinds. This doesn't just apply to people with disabilities, but to people with all kinds of differences!

School Days

One of the opportunities you're probably most familiar with is the chance to go to school. This might seem like an opportunity you'd be glad to do away with sometimes! But school gives you the chance to learn many things, which can lead to many other opportunities as you get older. It can also give you the chance to meet many different people and make friends. This can also lead to new opportunities!

Many disability rights **activists** over the years fought for the opportunity to go to school. One notable activist was Judy Heumann. She had an illness called polio as a child and used a wheelchair the rest of her life.

Learn More

Because of her wheelchair, Judy Heumann (1947–2023) wasn't allowed to go to school until she was in the fourth grade. Because of the ADA and other laws today, this is now illegal, or against the law.

Judy Heumann fought to go to school in more ways than one. She later fought for and won her teaching license in New York. She worked for the rights of those with disabilities in many ways throughout her life.

In the Classroom

The opportunity to go to school is, of course, important. But once you're there, you also need the opportunity to get an education! People with disabilities may need different sorts of accommodations to do this in a fair and effective way. There are many kinds of disabilities, and some people have more than one, so they might need a combination of accommodations.

A student who is hard of hearing may need to sit at the front of the classroom to better hear their teacher. A student with **sensory** issues might need to take a test in a different **environment** than other students.

You won't always know when a classmate has a disability-related accommodation. It's up to them if they want to tell anyone.

Learn More

Accommodations in the classroom can include changes in how teachers present **information** to students, how students **respond**, the time students need to work, the environment, and how lessons are planned.

Disability Differences

Even when you have a disability yourself, it might be hard to understand why other people need other kinds of help to reach for their opportunities. Some people even get upset with this. Why does one classmate get a printed copy of class notes when everyone else has to take notes themselves? Is that fair?

But you don't know if that classmate has an issue like dysgraphia. This is a disorder that affects someone's ability to write. It doesn't mean they're not working hard just like you are. They just need different help to get to the same place.

Learn More

If you or a friend has a disability, you've probably heard these three letters together: IEP. This stands for "**individualized** education program." This is a plan for how you learn.

Dyslexia is somewhat like dysgraphia, affecting how people deal with language. Dyscalculia involves the ability to do math and work with numbers.

For the Future

Opportunities aren't just about the present: they're about the future. The opportunity to go to school and get a good education leads to opportunities for jobs and careers later. Most workplaces, like schools, are required by the law to make sure people with disabilities have a chance at these jobs and the accommodations they need to do them well.

But that's what opportunities are: chances. The rest is up to you! It's important to know your rights so you can take advantage of the chances before you, whether they're a chance to learn, work, or play. What do *you* want to do?

Some playgrounds have different things to play on to accommodate those with disabilities. The opportunity to play is important too!

Glossary

access: The ability to use or enter something.

accommodation: Something supplied that is useful and handy.

activist: Someone who acts strongly in support of or against an issue.

ally: A person associated with another for support or a common purpose.

employer: A person or business that employs someone, or hires them for a job.

environment: The conditions that surround living things (including people) and affect the way they live.

individualize: To make something adapted to one person, or individual.

information: Knowledge or facts about something.

neurodiversity: Differences in the way the brain processes information.

respond: To do something as a reaction to something that has happened or been done.

sensory: Having to do with the senses.

transportation: A way to move from one place to another.

For More Information

BOOKS

Avis, Heather. *Different—A Great Thing to Be!* Colorado Springs, CO: WaterBrook, 2021.

Heumann, Judith, and Kristen Joiner. *Rolling Warrior: The Incredible, Sometimes Awkward, True Story of a Rebel Girl on Wheels Who Helped Spark a Revolution.* Boston, MA: Beacon Press, 2021.

Levy, Janey. *What Happens When I Have a Learning Difference?* Buffalo NY: Powerkids Press, 2024.

WEBSITES

Learning Problems
kidshealth.org/en/kids/learning-disabilities.html
The KidsHealth site explains learning disabilities and some ways to deal with them.

Your Rights Under the Americans with Disabilities Act (ADA)
www.verywellhealth.com/americans-with-disabilities act-5220487
Learn more about the ADA and your rights here.

Publisher's note to educators and parents: Our editors have carefully reviewed these websites to ensure that they are suitable for students. Many websites change frequently, however, and we cannot guarantee that a site's future contents will continue to meet our high standards of quality and educational value. Be advised that students should be closely supervised whenever they access the internet.

Index